Tomorrow
Ruined Today

RARE BIRD

Los Angeles, Calif.

Tomorrow
Ruined Today

Brett Lloyd & Ryan Kent

THIS IS A GENUINE RARE BIRD BOOK
PUBLISHED IN ALLIANCE WITH DEAD BOOKS PUBLISHING

Rare Bird Books
453 South Spring Street, Suite 302
Los Angeles, CA 90013
rarebirdlit.com

Cover Artwork by Diogo Soares

FIRST TRADE PAPERBACK ORIGINAL EDITION

Rare Bird Books Subsidiary Rights Department
453 South Spring Street, Suite 302
Los Angeles, CA 90013

Set in Dante
Printed in the United States

10 9 8 7 6 5 4 3 2 1

Publisher's Cataloging-in-Publication Data available upon request.

BRETT LLOYD

BRETT LLOYD is a native of Virginia Beach. He is the author of *Deception of Change*, *Hateburn*, and *Hour of Man*, and is the frontman for Pillbuster, Mammoth Black, and Down Again.

Thank you to everyone for everything. You know who you are and you know who you are not.

I'm ok with you not being here
I'm ok with the silence
It doesn't fuck with me anymore
I don't sit and stew in my grave
I realized the difference between
Want and need
What people may want are superficial to the make believe lives they live
What people need is to learn to accept things and move on
I'm ok with you not dying in front of me
The way everything was everyone's fault
The war that you would place in my hands every day of the people that
    didn't agree with you
The take and take and take and fucking take
There is no more to give except the silence it deserves
I'm ok

I hated you
The thought of you
Pressing me
Judging me
Giving me more and more reasons
To walk away
Until I became you
I grew into mold
No more excuses to not be what you are
No more hiding to what I have become

I feel empty now

Flowers in her hair
Glowing from every tortured angle
Muted smile and painted eyelids
Cascading bruises down her arm
"Can you hold me" she asked
I started looking around
Looking in her eyes I replied "Yes, but not forever"
She nodded
Walking towards me she spit blood into the grass
"Love is hard" she said
I acknowledged with a smirk
"Love is what you make it" I said as I walked closer to her
She nodded

Can I ask you a question
Do the feelings ever fade
Do they somehow completely go away
I need them to

The reminder of things make living this life very difficult
The constant feeling of feeling
The steady flow of emotion
Does it ever get easier
To let go
I need to let go

Approach the reproach
Destination is a headless moment
Where you sway your body to and fro
The music stops as the eyes cleanse your soul
Right through you they go
Toward something you've left behind
The grand disaster
Such distaste and passion
Evolution grows in moments that make you die
Mind relapses to distant memory
Distant illusions that you thought were real
You're struggling now
You never have before
Let go
Let your body sway from the noose
To and fro
Let your hands collapse
Breath gets shorter
You evolve into another state of being
Another sense of life

Dreams
I still have them
Far and away
My mind chases them
I remember all the times I thought I knew you
For what you were and what you were without
A holding of sorts
A mind erased
That look you use to give
When everyone and everything seemed to matter
Your funeral was open casket
Eyes closed
Hands clasped
I notice a small flower pinned on your dress
Your hair was nice
I can recall our last conversation
It is a moment that greets me every day
The look of good bye on both our faces
No one was there but us
But when I remember it
It's like someone took a picture
Dreams
I still have them
Far and away
My mind chases them
I remember all the times I thought I knew you

Chalkboard

Inviting dream
Writhing down the lamp shade
Turning off the light and seeping inside of you
Compiled realm
Naughty pleasures
Satisfying the hunger of denial
Destined intrusion to the mystic voyage
Oh, life and its deadly unmistakable hands of fate
To the nocturnal, the quiet bowing of this head is for you
Where is the piece that binds it all
In the hands that collapse in mine
In the body of love where upon entering is a defining pleasure
The chase deceiving
The catch inevitable
To the kingdom and its high rewards, I give toast
Distilled wine pouring from lovers mouths
She greets me under the table and acts out her notions of forgiveness
Lusting, so that I too may even crave
Confusion mounts a steady horse
In the back of my mind
Paralyzing fear grips my skull
Shall the cloth they put around my eyes be tight
In dreaded dreams I have died
Terrible and fallen deaths become my darkest reality
To speak is indescribable
Never has satisfaction ever distasted me
Befallen warriors
I wear your skin as I walk your graves
In a consciousness, I am not far from drowning my sorrow
I plead guilty on all accounts
Encased in your doubt I swallow my insides
Coming closer and drifting forward toward away
Reminding not to slip
Farther back down I go
Deep depths into the catacomb, I climb down the spiral staircase
Deep breaths and heavy footsteps
Blood and oil ignite to this bodies fuse

Intrude, none the lesser may
Mistakes many, yet far from breaking apart
Sick and healthy meanings combine to everlasting doubt
If the scenery has suited your vision
Then carry out your plastic memories of trust
Into the divided conquering of soulless jesters, I find you without eyes
Escaped into the Everest fields
Where gold and stardom hold delight
From a passing of deep regards, into the meadow you find me consulting
    my wounds
Come down Repunzal, with mask and all
Chariot I rode here, yet I walked very far
Chiseled remains my being, I become one with the bricks in your castle
    walls
Statue features
Statue graves unjustly forgotten
Weeds and soil torment my body inside of many frail graves
Fear, embrace my enthusiasm
Create me whole
Only to break down to weep eroded rivers, which you walk across later in
    life
Cloaked in forged darkness
Seeking the vessel where you hope to live and eventually destroy
My body is tired and very week, please do not apologize
A blooded man
With light skin and pale blue eyes
What was the beginning is now the end
A sunken skull with still fragments of blonde hair
Is all that is left now to remind
Yet, those fire filled blue eyes still remain in tact

♦♦♦

Configure the extinction
Corpses walking with pain unhindered
Nonetheless, you still make me aroused and obliged to your naked body
Now to your thoughts
Your thrusting pelvic perversions
I will stake the claim you offer

In this game, we will have the heads of lions
With skins of jackals
Uniting the difference to make perfect erection
In the lost ways, we shall find each other
A way of acknowledging the past, so forgotten
A way of truce between
Erotic fascination of guilt
I survive with you in mind
I keep the barrel loaded, with silver bullets to pretend
Have the dreams come too heavy for your shoulders to hold
My darling light seekers in dismay
Disdain these thoughts; I call out for you to leave me unanswered
Breathing has replaced living
On a scale I tip off the sides, yet I reach to grasp hold
Holding on with pain unbearable, my fingers break off and I fall into space
I have come to realize that you and I were to be here in this moment
May we never meet and know that it was meant to be that way
To search a whole life for perfection drawn incomplete
I grieve silently for you
For that has been my quest as well
For the ones that in which in order to live they have grown to except
I condone you, but I will not recondition my flaws
Like a cheetah on the run, I will get away or die
Looking around at these exhausting surroundings
With all of my cards dealt and with my possessions lost
I mockingly look at each face around me and make my final wager
Lungs are pulling in more air
Slowly my eyes dilate
No one could ever play my part in the play
Sunken eyes and alcohol coated breath
Just tell me who I am to you
To reunite what I was with what you claim me to be
Laughter is the only thing that has saved me since the last time we talked
I have laughed so hard that blood has rushed out of my eyes and nose
I see you staring blank and pretending not to wonder
A fairytale it was and will be
Till the end makes its final desperate act
With open arms and tormented judgment, I stand and wait for deliverance

◆◆◆

I refuse to apologize
As empty and suspicious that I am
As afraid and dismayed as you are
This drowning and restless life
Has caused me more pain than I could ever explain
These eyes that you look upon hold back so much
    that at times life is unbearable
I have died long ago
I belong to another age of time already abandoned each time you speak
I belong to the ones already deceived to be alive
Among these souls and spirits
I live unlike the rest
Stumbling around in the darkness,
I found my mask and glued it to my face
I am born only to grieve
For the children of this earth
For all that walk this face and trample on this soil
I will walk away from you
I hold no bonding remarks to your flesh
I am a ghost to your causes that even you will not understand;
    yet, I ask you
For what may the saved one have?
Glorious in entitled states where persecution rests asleep
I awaken the jury to crucify the judge
Grave thoughts taunt this sanctuary
Alive in the dungeon of life
I forward the matter into the hands of fate
I look the absolute in the eyes of victims
    screaming and reaching out in pain
To take a mind and bend it
Makes me difficult to ascertain
A troubled warrior hung by rope in the forest of illusion
Inapt to fate
A beautiful waterfall of blood and tears
    gracefully moistens the ground so dry
Smearing the paintings in delicate fashion
Slowly watching them ruin, I was wiping my wounds across their surface

Trying to create a Picasso with fragments from my mind
I hover over the souls
They watch me circle them, terrified as to what I might do
I extend their limbs and lay my body on top of them
Sweet women with such desire to unmask me
Hopeless, they make me a victim
I pretend like they do
In a lovers voice they depict love and admiration
In a lover's trance, I do the same
Difficult in making me speak my silence
So darling they are
They help me keep grounded to the world that breathes

Tonight replenishes the hurt
The guilty fall to the ground
Sickness and hate is all that controls, all that matters
Destiny walked away
I'm hurt and disgusted now
Help me stay immune to you

Ambition

Lay down
I will show you what it's like
Take your clothes off
Put your face near mine
Your uncovered flesh reveals my intentions
Relax your body as I climb in and deep
Don't worry you can put your mask on when you leave
I'll still be here
You cannot deny me anymore
I want to see your face when this all over
Come on now; just follow me with your eyes
Play the game with me

Death Trip

I promised you so many things as I slit your throat. Sweet revenge mixed with the rebirth of my violence. Toward you, your acts and deeds of thin lies scolded. Etched on your forehead is the dignity you lost.

All of your Heroes are dead.

They feed your courage with weakness in tiny pills.

They come in black suits. They have oilcans in their hands. They come to spill the oil, light the match and point at the differences between you and what they stand for. They chose you because they like the sound of your voice; they want to hear that beautiful voice scream.

You want to let go of the pain. But the pain never lets go of you.

You look in the mirror as you hear the world chant your name. You make it look so easy, the way you make it look so good. It's all coming back to you. Firing a bullet of hell trusted insulin right into your veins. You sink back in your easy chair thinking that the war is over, that the new land isn't far from where you think you are. Your new land has already been destroyed.

You have no sides to the situation. As you think about forever, you think about your next move forward. Your easy chair is now stained with blood from your veins which talk and humiliate you. Time and time again, you lose yourself in drugs.

The drugs rape you. You always beg for more. You like the feeling of leaving the world, but only just for a while. Then you come back and circle over our heads with a new found wisdom that speaks to you and only you. Yet you try to share the moment. I console you. I understand you. I want to leave this world too, but my trigger finger isn't what it used to be.

Idol

The fearless warrior
With ugly eyes and facet hair
A terrified leader
A faithless hero
Wearing your crown of glory upon your magical head
Drawn, are symbols of war upon your face
Taste the blood from victims slain by misfortune who greet you
Golden boy, with a smile to pretend
You fucking coward
I demand you to face me
Inside the hollowness of fear
Surviving is your only option
Your Hell is filled with mirrors
Depicting every moment forgotten in your life
Plagued by regret
You will know remorse
Memories elude the senses
You are trapped in a retrospect of things that cannot change
Grab a chair
We will sit and draw blood from our lips with
conversation
No alibis to highlight the questioning of certainty
Calm and relax your frustration, you are home now
With some other distaste and no defiant belonging

Her

I thought about you today
I thought about ripping off your dress
Sliding my hands down your stomach and into your underwear
About taking my tongue and licking
Filling my mouth with your juice
Making you fragile
Making you beg

I will look into your eyes when I go into you
I want to see the moment that you let go of sanity
Let go of everything

You feel good underneath me
Your body is shaking as I lift your legs in the air
Back and forth
You're screaming for a God
This won't be the last time
It's never the last time

You were nervous around me afterward
Like I knew you almost too well
I just wanted to get your scent off of my clothes

Doubtful Ambition
In the corner by the clock
Closer to the wall
Come a little more
Now walk closer
Good, right there, close your eyes
Feel with your hands
The empty feeling in your heart
Growing heavy, starting to settle
Feel the absence of everything around you
Turn and put your nose against the feeling
Clinch your fists so tight that your knuckles turn white
Wrap your thoughts around the hopelessness
Create a balance and distance between
Subtract yourself from the absence
Within this realm of evolution
Within the pure distrust
Place your back against the wall
And as you look into the world you see with your new eyes
Run away into the shadow of a life gone by
Find the road to suggestion
Go forth into the new happening
Awaken yourself from the dreams and start creating reality
For it is what one needs
What one wants
For if, you have the legs to stand
You have to find the heart to continue

Raging city
Screaming warpath heroes

Tumbling into the noises
Headlights flicker against your eyes
With nonsense driven insanity
The Moon, lights up these streets of rage
My consciousness, far from normal occupants
Alive inside the war drum
Killing the innocence by numbers
I wish you could come closer
Fellow membership inside the ever-present sightlessness
We steady the pace
War symbols drawn on our faces
I throw you against the passing cars Deep colors bleed
Onto your flesh the colors fade
Wipe the colors away
Look in the other direction

Same breath
Same example
Retire into the battle hung mysteries
We fall away in the outcome
Deep voices scream
Onto your mind the voices decline
Hide the voices
Hear other changes in disposition
Same breath
Same example
Deep colors bleed

No one has a name
No one has a face

Only gimmicks
To satisfy the crowd
Only masks
With painted tears to show remorse
Pieces are only glued together to make a fit
There is no emotion because emotion is dead
There are no wars to show ugliness unless it is made from human fit
There are no flowers to show compassion unless needed to kill beauty
    once again

There is only the present state of the world
A world that shows money is equal to everlasting power and desire
A world where plastic replaces the ugliness

Humans are an imitation product
Standing idle while we have everything totally stripped away from us,
    and who we used to be

I have found you
In the songs of the past

In the moments gone
In the flashes of light that are demonstrated

Will I be replaced by the situation at hand?
A toy to the monster within you

Have I lost self-control?
You waved goodbye as you saw it leave

From your fingers I slip away
I fade into the background scenery

And, yet you apologize to my face and body
To my unwashed and dirty soul

Tell me how you are different

Face to face
Smiling out
Lose of reality
Touching my skin
Pieces of memory fade
I cannot recall exactly what happened
Death-invoked sense of destruction
I slowly dissolve
Into nothing
To go forward is to always look back
She left me yesterday
Or maybe the day before
I'm not sure anymore
All I know is the emptiness that has greeted me since
All I know is the broken mirror that stands shattered before me
I sit and stare at these bare walls
The empty room inside of a shell of a life lived and now vanished
Alone in comfort
Empty spaces of a house where things used to be
   and where beings used to dream
I can remember conversations and laughter
I remember nights of running away from the situation
I remember dreams of breaking away and returning to my real life
Trips and journeys to nowhere in-between
Nights of isolation and desperation to break free of the torment of living
She left me
Here alone I stand
Here alone, I call out her name and whisper goodbye
Needed time to end
I climb in as she climbs out
Her ways of taking me seriously grows thin
Her tired naked thoughts call out to me
Silently she awaits my approval of acceptance
She needs no invitation for ideas as passion grows
She drains all life as it is given for her pleasure
Remembrance of existence shrouds unshed tears from her eyes
Never have I been as afraid as to where life shall take me
Far away today
Closer to her tomorrow

We need the silence always
As we grow further and further apart
Starving Actor
I come to you in a storm of soft whispers
Rolling smoke off my lips into words that tempt you
You smile and place your hand between your thighs
I see how you starve
How you desire
You already feel a sense of love for me
You know nothing about me
You love the appearance
You love how I can put the shine on real quick
It is all an act
I learned how to be pleasing and how to pretend
You love how I can appreciate you with just one look
Yet, I fear for you
I am a man of many different flaws
Within this mind are things that you will never understand
I will watch as you walk out the door

Exhausted Dreams
Icicles stretch across fingertips
Supplying the neurotic visions
Spine slopes down the chair
Hair falls to mid back
Eyes suppress across the expression
Time is indenting lines of depression

Quickening and crawling the phrase
Hold on to this notion

Dreams shatter the skull
Stomach heaves in and out
Exhaustion fuels sweat down the face
Mask collapses to the floor
Widening smile
Indifferent tactics to the make believe

The game gets harder
Fear begins to make it impossible

Night storms by slowly
Temptations wearing through and out
Heart is racing
Nose smells the charred flesh
Hardening to a crisp
Lips splinter against the face

Colors reflect rampant on the skin
Noises are not heard but acknowledged
Denial fuses the ends together
Arms move violently to the rhythm of lost expectations
Back blisters against the chair
Daylight seems so far away

Body embraces itself
Walls act as shields

Pictures elude the senses
The images retire
Invisible creatures consume

Inside, the heart dies of frustration
Deep penetrating glances
The mirror bends in

Chair crashes to the floor
Body goes with it
Crawling away
Hands and knees burn
Head bowed down
Trying to understand the happening
Cameo
Colors smear
Blood has no scent
Pressure builds high above
The ground shakes
Hands and knees
A crawl for shelter
Down hidden paths
Running to seek refuge
Devoid of life and into the past
What lies ahead?
None shall know
Though, I must travel
Through the valley of wounded sorrow

Tempting Resolve
The picture was clear
Just a pure painted picture on the walls of Hell
I was trying to ease my mind
Forget about the tasks at hand
Yet, just another victim I was
Standing motionless and blank with every emotion stirring inside of me
I denied its touch
A painting stirring with years and centuries past
We are the things it hides
Sheltered and abstract
Vacant and pretending
The Revenge of Ever-present Change
Stare and devour
Present refusal
Bleached thoughts
Cry out for forgiveness
Piece of mind runs away
Second guessing the situations
I fall
Into sins of betrayal
Never the same again
Cold darkness
Soothe these terrified eyes
Fade with these thoughts
Total desolation
What was I
Just what was I trying to find
In darkness I see before my closed eyes
Just what was I trying to need?
In confinement deep inside my mind
Just what was I trying to touch?
In seclusion, with hands bound behind my back
Just what was I trying to taste?
In shadows,
with my teeth drawing blood from my tongue
Just what was I?
In darkness
I sifted through your ashes tonight

I found things that I never noticed before
I came across old letters
Old pictures
Old times when everything seemed
Where there was still a dream
Where there was still peace between us
The moments that kept what we had alive
I remember our last conversation
You were so illustrated in how you were talking to me
Wondering how I was
If I was sleeping
If I missed you
If I found someone to stand beside
To lay beside
Another dream to pretend
You sounded so hurt
You seemed like you cared
I wish you would have acted like that when we use to exist
There is nothing here for you now
You use to call me a ghost
But now that I have become a ghost
You don't like the vision
You were right
I will say that
I will stay who I am
I seemed to change into what you wanted me to be
The sad part is that I got use to being what you created
I got use to the idea of just drifting beside you
You have no idea how much that hurt

♦♦♦

I still remember some of the good times
The different and lonely places that I took you while we were together
The calming thought is that we could both walk away still
Not that there is not scarring
It was hard
But it has gotten easier
Sometimes I relive the moments

31

I can see the dreams we had
But sometimes I relive the moments
I can see the emptiness that surrounded me
I lived in a void
I lived in a place where everything around me seemed to exist
And I got to pretend
I got the watch from a far
With my own dreams not shared
My own thoughts sitting vacant
I was dying quick
Rendering in the afterglow
Making cuts into my eyes
While wrinkles of age deepened into my face

♦♦♦

So next time we speak
If there is a next time
Don't be surprised if I say nothing
Don't judge me
Don't pretend to know me
Don't say something that you think is brilliant to try to apologize
In fact I would rather just pass by
We can look in each others eyes
And I will say nothing
I will pass by unnoticed
Indifferent
Not dreaming
Not pretending
Not apologizing
Not caring
Not hopelessly hanging on
Not regretting
Not trying to recapture
Not embracing the idea of maybe
I will just pass by
And just like before we met
You will not know me
And just like when we were together
You will not know me

So here is the boy become man. Swimming in the changing tide. His reality has escaped him at last. Insanity, he pleads guilty on all accounts. A traveler that fell victim. To the ever-present change of circumstance. Immersed in fierce doubt that any of this is real.

He confides to himself. In the basking glow of certainty. That he has at last found new land. From the tide he has broke free and steps his feet ashore. An unholy land has dissolved him. He is scrutinized by his actions. On a cross they lay him for the wake of his breathless body. Yet, he stopped breathing years ago. His ravaged and tortured soul has just remained for the cowards to cast down their burdens.

Alive in the brink of death he has astounded the on lookers in dismay. The skin of the fallen have laid haste into his body. He combines the blood with his own to make him more forgiving to the cause. Wearing glory upon his head and stepping beyond the roses laid at his feet. He turns in your direction. For guidance and for control to the disease of life.

A single tear sheds down the face of the absent-minded host. The prelude of things to come as everything snaps and spins out of control. He rests beside his loses. Covered in blankets of ash from the fire where they burned him. Into the sky he raises his broken glass to give toast to a new beginning. He remembers his beginning. He remembers the downfall of his choking spirit.

Will he lash out into the empty night and hold true to his promise? Will he stay compromised and disdained in the wreckage? Hopefully just long enough. So that the feelings never show. So that the days that outnumber him grow inside the swelling, raging carnival that becomes his dreams. And his reaction will be just. His emotion will be just. And you will hear him screaming from the inside of your skull. And when you lay to rest your tired spirit, you will feel the beating of his heart slowing to a steady rhythm of decline. Then there will be nothing. Nothing but the blank expression upon your worn and broken face. The mask he will keep for his collection. Your dreams he will own for the time in which you spent rejecting his idea of grace and peace.

A war drum begins to wander its sounds through the valley of the hopeless. I must subtract myself from the presentation of the gift that lies at your feet broken and still wrapped with the hope of being whole again. Good night. I bid you a peace that I have never known.

I sit in a room
In a chair
With straps on my ankles and arms
My head bowed down in forgiveness
My body naked and bruised
Blood trickles from my eyes
My heart is racing
My mind is questioning everything
I hear voices in the background
Screaming
Threatening
I try to open my eyes
I can't
I can't move anymore
The muscles in my body have reached a point of retire
I feel footsteps coming closer to me
Who has come to my aid
Someone lifts my head
There are no words
I feel them breathing in my face
Hot air
Smell of candy
They hold my head by my hair
With a clinched fist and rough idea
They let go
My head drops back down
I feel the footsteps walk away
No voice
Nothing
I hear a faint sound of a door close
I can feel the muscles tearing inside my body
My stomach is turning from lack of food
My mouth is so dry that I can taste the blood from my lips
I have no idea what day it is
I have no idea how long I have been here
All I remember is distant thoughts
I'm not sure any of it was real
I have this disturbing thought that I'm not alone in here
I can feel that someone is here with me

Staring at me
Believing in me
Consoling me
But there is just the feeling
Just the hope
Hope
What hope is left for me now
What is the meaning of all of this abuse
I have been so many places
Seen so many people come and go
So many things I have taken and given up
For what
For what cause
I guess mine as well as yours
But here I sit
No tears
No remorse
Not a shadow of a doubt
Not a razor in my fist
Not a death for me to seek
I just sit here
I recall the changes in my mind
The smell of spring
The colors of fall
The heat of summer
The coldness of winter
All seasons
All reasons
My life has been a secession of lives
Gathered around different seasons in which I grew up and grew against
I have had my time in the Sun
My time in the cold dark disease of excuses
But I have taken things for what they are
And for what they aren't
Different seasons
That is what makes up my life
Changes in climate
Changes in thought
Changes in the appearance

Changes in the soul
Sometimes I have given up on what I have believed in
Sometimes I have given up on myself
Sometimes I didn't even notice
I have played the ghost
I have played the jester
I have been the King
I have been anything and anyone you could imagine
But through it all
I have been myself
I haven't disowned the true thought
In fleeting moments
I never have walked others paths to find rebellion
I waged my war in my own way
My battle cry has been my own
No weapons
No flag of honor
No need for help
No apologies to give
No reason to not carry out the fight
I have never needed a reason
I have my own
My own thoughts
My own opinions
I am my own executioner
My own judge and jury
I understand that at times I will not understand
But there is always a reason for every piece of my life that have created
    this puzzle
But here I am
Sitting in this room
The waiting room
With no voice left
And no one to cry out to

TO BE CONTINUED…

RYAN KENT

RYAN KENT is the author of three collections of poetry: *Hit Me When I'm Pretty*, *This Is Why I Am Insane*, and *Poems For Dead People*. He is the microphone player for the thrash band Murdersome, and contributes to Ozy.com and *RVA Magazine*. He lives Cali-sober in Richmond, Virginia.

Thank you to my family, to loved ones, and to the people who taught me to write.

I DON'T NEED THE WORLD ANYMORE

cars parked in the field
after the lot was full

there was rain

they tore up the grass
following the hearse

one car got stuck

an old man and a boy
pushed the front

its tires spun nowhere

the old man fell down
yelled at the boy

we watched

sometimes
it's just like

that

HOW DO YOU TAKE YOURS?

she keeps trying to add cream and sugar
i tell her i don't want it

it's ok
you'll like it

people normally take cream and sugar

i tell her i don't want it   a g a i n

why are you like that

if it makes you happy
put the cream and sugar in
i say

she does
smiles and stirs

i'm sure
you'll like it

i go outside
have a cigarette

it's still raining

after that one's done
i have another

go back inside
sit down

i don't know why
you must smoke

it'll kill you
she says

the server comes over
doesn't look at us

puts the wrong plates down
walks away

i call to her
                n o t h i n g

when i turn back
she's chewing

yours looks good
she says

it's not what we ordered
i tell her

next time i come here
i'm getting what you got

she starts playing
with her phone

i go outside
have a cigarette

it's still raining

after that one's done
i have another

MORE OF THE SAME

she kept folded napkins
in her car's cup holders

her mother
had also done this

both of them kept
used tissues in
their coat pockets

they were a lot alike

she said
i think the picture is too high
in the small bedroom

      i thought it looked nice
              i said

i have to have nick hang the mirror
then he can hang a small picture
under the picture that's
hung too high in the
small bedroom

      i can hang those
            i said

i had a man this morning
put a railing down the stairs
because donnie said
i could fall
and the man left
      a mess

tomorrow the cable man
will be here between 1 and 3
and nick will be here at 4
to hang the pictures

i watched her cat flick his tail
on the back of the sofa

and you'll be here to move the tv at 6
so that nick can hang the mirror
because donnie said the wall in
the dining room looks empty

nick died the following
morning

the man hung the
pictures and the mirror

i didn't come over
to move the tv

donnie called

STORM OF THE CENTURY

the boy came
down
the stairs
again

opened the
front door

we were sitting there

wind blowing
everything   a r o u n d

is the hurricane here yet
he asked

it isn't
said his father

is it coming

probably not
l i a m
it's just gonna
get windy

the boy accepted this
closed the door
went back upstairs

you know he's up there
watching the news
waiting for the storm
of the century
his   f a t h e r
said

probably so
i said

down the block
a big woman
argued loudly
with another
big woman

they began to tussle
with each other
in the street
as the wind
picked up

a lawn chair
blew over
we waited

OUT IN THE WORLD AGAIN

i remember when
she left him

he waited in
the long lines

stayed
up nights

she never
called

i see him
from time to time

a little grayer
thinner

takes care
of his mother now

kind of a shut in

MONET

three cars up
a minivan merged
into the funeral procession

county police
blocked off the next lane
with blue lights

the minivan driver
had painted itself
into our corner

all of us together
proceeded onto the interstate
east to the cemetery

we watched the minivan
take the first exit
somewhere

squinted our eyes
as it peeled down
the off ramp

i'd come to understand
the significance of this matter
the farther removed from it i was

a painting that looks
better from over   t h e r e

CAN YOU SEE HEAVEN?

she still dresses nice
goes to the salon
gets touchups to her hair

and she loves to go
there to see bryan

i guess here
i could quote

rimbaud or rilke
          or
                    richard hell
but that's just

bullshit

and half of us
have felonies
and didn't
finish college
a n y w a y

here we are
at the glaucoma specialist
                a g a i n

the receptionist says
mom is dressed
very nice and mom
really is dressed
very nice

and her hair
also looks very nice

i know she's gotten old
but gotten old in a way
only   i   n o t i c e

while   they see
a nice old lady

i see   my mother

looking for a
                blurry blue
                heaven
                every day

and I know life
is likewise

bullshit

just something else
she can't see
                either

SIX FIGURES

then i stopped
counting the ants
after i killed them

thought about
the 6 people i knew
who had died in the
last 6 months

i remembered
      from somewhere
            that ants and bees
    and even termites
bury their own

         but never count them

only people
count them

THE FINAL STAGE

so doris day died
and so did tim conway
shit even chewbacca died

it isn't any different
than any other year
just different
p e o p l e

point is
god isn't
h u m a n
or doesn't act
h u m a n
and you can't
blame   g o d
for that

because
p e o p l e
don't act
h u m a n
anymore
e i t h e r

and
g o d
hasn't
changed

sliding around
saying be well
saying you're
an activist

doesn't make it
any truer than it
was an hour before
you decided to buy

that yoga mat

just some other clot
with a guilty conscience
thinking paper straws
will get them into

h e a v e n

now scientists are saying
one million species
are expected
to go extinct
in the next
ten years

and the only people
who give a goddamn
are the a s s h o l e s
buying yoga
mats

                              perry cleared his
                              throat to speak

                              but walter just
                              continued

like i've seen
restaurant owners
run their businesses
into the ground
after they
r e a l i z e
it's over

listening to lawrence welk
    drinking their bar's inventory
        firing the wait staff

        and doing it out of
h o p e l e s s n e s s

or just run of the mill

s p i t e
i guess
fuck all
is in our
genetic
makeup

        walter took
        a n o t h e r
        v o d k a s h o t
        wiped his mouth

speaking of
f u c k a l l

the other day
i saw a guy
smoking
a cigarette
through his
t r a c h e

filter right up to the h o l e   O

and if that ain't
f u c k a l l
then i don't know
what is

        we all looked at walter

        i missed drinking

MY MOTHER'S GLAUCOMA

when i looked down
i noticed her toenails
were very long

one curled over
it's toe

what's that   i pointed down

i can't see to cut them   she said

that's why you're always wearing shoes

yes

i got the toenail clippers
from the green jar
in the medicine cabinet
(she told me where they were)

i cut her toenails

i never could've done
that for daddy   she said

oh it probably didn't make
any difference   i said

they were like concrete   she said

i went to the kitchen
to wash my hands

some things
are like
concrete

CHAMPION

i was there when her father died

bottom of the ninth
game seven   the p e n n a n t
two outs bases loaded
francisco cabrera line drive base hit left field
justice scores
bream rounds third
throw to the plate
safe

atlanta

it wasn't the first time i'd
seen him asleep
he was dreaming
moving his arms
above the pillow
rolling lightly
side to side
in the hospice bed
like shadowing
his shadow

lost the year before
to minnesota

tenth inning
game seven   w o r l d   s e r i e s
gene larkin first pitch single left center field
gladden scores
jack morris   thirty-six years old
complete game
shut out

twins

she'd taken off his signet ring
fourteen carat gold

a capital c in old english
on the face

handed it to me

it's on my finger now

old men and their rings

THIS I'LL TELL YOU BROTHER

albert said louise
had never worked
a day in her life

the following afternoon
louise decided to wash
their pontiac

albert went out there
with a camera
to get proof

l o u i s e

behive
hairdo

pouncey
sunglasses

yellow
mod dress

lilac flower
gloves

right there
in the driveway
with an old bucket
of soap water

he snapped it

didn't expect to see
her do that again

and she didn't expect
him to die at 48

but he did

then she died
like fifteen years
later

and that's what happened
with them

so

go ahead

get married

sometimes it's just washing the car

i may have that photo of louise

around here somewhere

EXPERIENCE THE DIVINE

down by the river
i looked at this rock

huddled around
a pile of others
like it

all of them
clean shaven
under water

ready
for this new day
like the last one

having
conceded
to it

a death

the jagged ones
sticking out of
the current

they don't know

it will always
end like this

the only river
they'll ever experience

each one
to be pushed
over

and
forgotten
as we
were

the divine

i have died
many times
this way
and lived
to be a
smooth
old man

THERE'S A SONG IN THERE

i was in line at the craft store buying a frame

a man in dirty clothes
came   up
handed me a dollar

     not trying to bother you
           he said

but my friend is addicted to crack
and he's out there playing the guitar

i looked at the dollar

he's been sober a week and i just want
to give him some positive reinforcement

he walked off
repeated the same thing
to a lady looking at
magic markers

i paid for the frame
went outside

the guy was sitting
on a bench
playing the guitar

wasn't any good

i put the dollar in his cup

let me play you a better one
          he said

        it was an original

the man who gave me the dollar walked up

we did not   a c k n o w l e d g e

at some point the tune ended

thanks a lot   i said

he nodded at the dollar in the cup

i appreciate it

                    walked to my car

i can't p l a y
the g u i t a r

  either

A COUPLE OF BURRITOS

she's walking over

to our table

checkered yellow bandana

matching her

        hi top   yellow vans
        tiny   black   shorts

says she's
shirley

takes
our burrito
order

it's the same thing here at
t h e   a c a p u l c o

off
calle
     l o i z a

as it is
most places
for girls her age
still trying

bless that child

i wear secondhand
clothes and forgot
to brush my teeth

we eat the burritos
go back to carlos's
apartment

i read my latest book

on the front porch alone
because i'm in san juan
and have an
e g o

tomorrow
i will catch a flight
2 4 0 0 miles

n o r t h

and a day
closer
to

3 7

my
older
friends
laugh
me
o f f

they say
i'm still
young

but
i'm already
thinking
about it
now

friends

so maybe
we're just talking about
two different things

HEY YOU GET YOUR DAMN HANDS OFF HER

carlos told me not to
go to the beach after dark

point your headlights
down there   he said

we were sitting
on a balcony
without
headlights

male hookers wait
in that tall grass and
they'll eat you whole

i lit the roach from the ashtray

thought about all the unsuspecting
men eaten alive on v a c a t i o n
right there in san juan

didn't need a time machine
to remember when
i too was eaten alive

but it wasn't by
a male prostitute
or a yellow tree boa
or a hole in the
world

just your average
run of the mill
white girl

ALL DOGS

the dog had been dead 5 years

her hair was still stuck down
beneath the 25 watt lightbulb
in the plastic lamp by his bed

it had been in many rooms since

the hair never cleaned out

a ziploc bag in his jewelry box
also contained this hair

when he finally did clean
inside the lamp
he regretted it

thought the change
would be good

n e c e s s a r y

he went back to the trash
to recover the hair
but saw it amongst the
hair of the new dogs

even with the flashlight

he knew he was
looking right at them

but couldn't tell
the difference

BIG PHARMA

they moved gilchrist
to the bullben
after the
all star break

in the off season
they put him on
medication

he came back
different

house
broken

stopped
spitting
at the fans

didn't hit
the batters
anymore

relied on
off speed
pitches

rationale

instead of
fastballs

and

pure
hate

hitters were
batting ted williams
against him

so the club
sent gilchrist
back to tampa

it happens like
that with pitchers
sometimes

they get in their
heads or   w o r s e

let someone else
get in their
heads

messes with
the mechanism

well shit
you know
what

it's getting
late

i gotta
take my pill
before bed

but you
wanna know
something

i can't help it

sometimes
after i shut
out the lights

get under
the blanket

i feel like i'm also
back in tampa

SHAVING LESSON

if you caught jack
on the right day

looked close enough

you could see
his beard was uneven

you can't get overzealous
with an electric razor

he said to me once

it's like a poem
or marriage
before sex

another sighting of jack
the sides would be reconciled

i see this gesture
most places now

at a traffic light

a woman in the passenger seat
of the jeep in front of me
shouts at the driver

i turn the radio down

the driver keeps quiet
she keeps shouting

i forgo the interstate
follow them down
arthur ashe blvd

scratch at the hair on my neck
maybe i'll try a beard

WEEDS

after his wife
moved out

he found
alcohol

started hosting
all nighters

fell asleep with a
cigarette

burned the
house up

and him too

it was in the
newspaper

i don't remember
his name though

just the house

when you drove
past it

the crabgrass in the
gravel driveway

fanned out

the same way smoke goes
room to room

asking for a ride
home

DRIVING SCHOOL

the camaro
had been parked
in the driveway
next door

always
beside
his
truck

for years

one night
i didn't see
her camaro

it wasn't there
the following
morning

or the night after
or the morning
after

just like that

the car was gone

he didn't bring it up
and i didn't ask

sometimes
he'd be smoking
a cigarette on his
front porch

looking out
at the field
across the street

waiting for
it to turn green

and

i never heard
him weep

may want to write that down

HITTING INSTRUCTOR

the house on eden drive had a deck
with a mound of gravel underneath

it opened out into the backyard
which grew trees
but little grass

most nights after school
he'd be down there

hitting gravel with
scrap particle board
or a sawed off piece of 2X4

if a rock made it
b o u n c e l e s s
across the creek
he considered it a homer

duke snider

gil hodges

down there
he'd hit their homers
for them

said it was
when he was
the happiest

didn't expect
to find himself
an old man

still looking for
the same satisfaction
with a different

swing

HOW DOES ONE NOT DRINK?

he said when he came home
from the war all he wanted to do
was fish

they kept asking him to play ball

some man said they
might quit asking

well fuck 'em   he said

after a while
ted agreed to play

gave the people
what they wanted

i laid in bed that night
listening to the
phone ring

she'd have come over
if i'd unplugged it

got in the shower
turned on the hot water

the phone continued
to ring and ring

after i ended it with alice
all i wanted to do
was drink

didn't even want
to write anymore

but a l i c e probably
had a bottle with her

and had likely
almost given up
calling by then

one of these days
i'd have to write
again anyway

so i answered
the phone

figured i'd
give the people
what they wanted

BOOM BAP

claude drums for ween
and is in the living room
singing into a microphone
playing an acoustic electric

there's a

                              dude playing keys
                                    dude on drums
                                        dude on bass

at some dude's house

                    down here
in   asheville   nc

              an old flannel couch
                is on the porch
                                        i sit

looking at other people's sky
                    their trees and brush
                    feel their free breeze

blow cigarette smoke into all
                    of it

WHAT WE DO WHEN WE PUKE

when we drove by
      she said

a lady had been

d   ecapitated

i s a w i t

two cars were all
smashed into
one another

right on
r o u t e
t h r e e

police cruisers
and fire trucks
were there

the rescue squad

my window
was down

and i have a
weak stomach

but
i looked
a n y w a y

it was lying
in the road

the woman's
head

i didn't
know her

after that
all anybody in the car
could talk about

was

j a n e
m a n s f i e l d

so now of course
whenever somebody
brings up

j a n e
m a n s f i e l d

instantly

i think of
that other
woman

her head

sideways
in the road

it just makes
me sick

and i liked

j a n e
m a n s f i e l d

DO NOT BEND

after the fact
we didn't get them developed

thought we'd get around to it

send them out
stamped and
addressed

to this uncle

that aunt

but never did

almost like
it never happened

the first time i mowed
my grandmother's grass

she watched me
from the kitchen window

then came outside

stepped a few feet
in front of the mower

pointed her finger
down at the grass
and walked forward

drawing an invisible line
for me to follow

so the cut
would be even

then it rained for two days
the fresh lines gone
by midweek

almost like

the cutting itself

had also

never happened

CREATIVE WRITING

galaraga would start
first base over mcgriff

lemke at second
put furcal over at ss
eddie mathews at third

chipper in left field
henry aaron in right

g u t says to play otis nixon in center
but dale murphy is more dependable

although
murphy isn't
a leadoff man

catchers are javier lopez and
eddie perez (explanation below)

still need a dh
for october

ok

mcgriff starts at first
galaraga is the dh

starting 5 man rotation

maddux   (comes with perez)

smoltz
glavine
spahn
nichols

bullpen of 10

wohlers   (pre steve blass)
sutter

burdette
avery
niekro
hudson
teherán
buhl
millwood
sain

bobby cox
is the s k i p p e r

wrote all
that down

hung it
on the wall

felt good
to dream

and then i
remembered

this one
january

seated with her in a
grocery store cafe

she removed
a typed letter
from her purse

read it

said it's over

for this reason
that reason

these reasons

all of which
were my doing

i moved out

her lawyer mailed me
a no fault divorce

i signed it

some time later
heard she'd
slid back
to her ex

which just
goes to show

you can dream up
a n y t h i n g
you want to

on paper

TO BE CONTINUED…